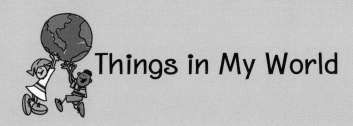

Things in My World

Things I Eat

Reading consultant:
Susan Nations, M.Ed.,
author/literacy coach/
consultant in literacy development

Please visit our web site at: www.garethstevens.com
For a free color catalog describing Weekly Reader® Early Learning Library's list
of high-quality books, call 1-877-445-5824 (USA) or 1-800-387-3178 (Canada).
Weekly Reader® Early Learning Library's fax: (414) 336-0164.

Library of Congress Cataloging-in-Publication Data

Things I eat.
   p. cm. – (Things in my world)
  ISBN-10: 0-8368-6810-2 — ISBN-13: 978-0-8368-6810-4 (lib. bdg.)
  ISBN-10: 0-8368-6817-X — ISBN-13: 978-0-8368-6817-3 (softcover)
  1. Food—Juvenile literature. I. Weekly Reader Early Learning Library (Firm). II. Series.
TX355.T44   2006
641.3—dc22   2006011468

This edition first published in 2007 by
Weekly Reader® Early Learning Library
A Member of the WRC Media Family of Companies
330 West Olive Street, Suite 100
Milwaukee, WI 53212 USA

Managing editor: Dorothy L. Gibbs
Art direction: Tammy West
Cover design and page layout: Kami Strunsee
Picture research: Diane Laska-Swanke
Photography: Gregg Andersen

Printed in the United States of America

1 2 3 4 5 6 7 8 9 10 09 08 07 06

Note to Educators and Parents

Learning to read is one of the most exciting and challenging things young children do. Among other skills, they are beginning to match the spoken word to print and learn directionality and print conventions. Books that are appropriate for emergent readers will incorporate many of these conventions while also being appealing and entertaining.

The books in the *Things in My World* series are designed to support young readers in the earliest stages of literacy. Children will love looking at the full-color photographs while also being challenged to think about words that name objects and how those words fit into a basic sentence structure. This integration allows young children to maximize their learning as they see how words and ideas are put together.

In addition to serving as wonderful picture books in schools, libraries, and homes, this series is specifically intended to be read within instructional small groups. The small group setting enables the teacher or other adult to provide scaffolding that will boost the reader's efforts. Children and adults alike will find these books supportive, engaging, and fun!

—Susan Nations, M.Ed., author, literacy coach,
and consultant in literacy development

bread

I eat **bread**.

peanut butter

I eat
peanut butter.

jelly

I eat **jelly**.

carrots

I eat **carrots**.

bananas

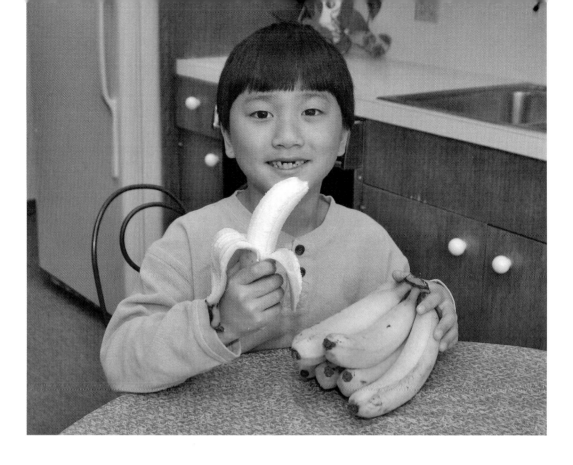

I eat **bananas.**

milk

I drink **milk.**

I eat these
things for lunch.